STAR FILES

Johnny Depp

Jane Bingham

Raintree

Chicago, Illinois

© 2006 Raintree
a division of Reed Elsevier Inc.
Chicago, Illinois

Customer Service 888-363-4266
Visit our website at
www.heinemannraintree.com

Originated by Modern Age
Printed and bound in China by South China
Printing Company

10 09 08 07 06
10 9 8 7 6 5 4 3 2 1

**Library of Congress Cataloging-in-
Publication Data**
Bingham, Jane.
  Johnny Depp / Jane Bingham.
     p. cm. -- (Star files)
  Includes bibliographical references and
index.
  ISBN 1-4109-1657-X (library binding--
hardcover)
  1. Depp, Johnny--Juvenile literature. 2.
Motion picture actors and actresses--United
States--Biography--Juvenile literature. I. Title.
II. Series.
  PN2287.D39B56 2005
  791.4302'8'092--dc22

2005005251

JB
DEPP, J
c. 1   1/07

Acknowledgments
The author and publisher are grateful to the
following for permission to reproduce
copyright material: Allstar (Cinetext
Collection) pp. **4**, **9** (b), **17** (t), **20**, **21** (l), **23**
(b), **23** (t), **25** (b), **30** (b), **31**, **38**; Allstar
Collection pp. **15** (b), **32** (r), **33**, **39** (b);
Allstarpl.com p. **21** (r); Corbis pp. **9** (t)
(Gianni Dagli Orti), **12** (SYGMA/Cardinale
Stephane), **14**, **29** (SYGMA/Picturescope
Internat), **30** (Stapleton Collection), **36**
(Bettmann); Getty Images (Photodisc) pp. **10**
(t), **15** (t), **37**; iStockPhoto pp. **7** (t) (Dan
Brandenburg), **17** (b) (Allen Johnson); Retna
Ltd pp. **24** (Steve Granitz), **27** (Sara De Boer),
28 (t) (Robert Frazier), **32** (l) (Robert Matheu),
36 (r) (Carmen Valdes); Rex Features pp. **5**
(Vinnie Zuffante), **6** (Camilla Morandi), **7** (b)
(Joyce Silverstein), **8** (Kip Rano), **10** (b)
(Richard Young), **11** (Richard Young), **13** (Karl
Schoendorfer), **16** (Ray Tang), **18** (SNAP), **19**
(SNAP), **22** (Pic Photos), **25** (t) (SNAP), **26**
(SNAP), **28** (b) (Crollalanza), **34**, **35** (Paul
Grover), **39** (t), **40** (Nils Jorgensen), **41** (b)
(Makey/Rooke), **41** (t) (Peter Brooker), **42** (C.
Warner Br/Everett), **43** (Peter Brooker).
Cover photograph reproduced with permission
of Rex Features (Vinnie Zuffante).

Quote sources: pp. **4**, **8**, **10**, **13**, **19**, **23**, **27**,
32, **34**, **38** *What's Eating Johnny Depp?* Nigel
Goodall, 2004; p. **29** http://www.ohjohnny.
net/quotes.html; pp. **37**, **42** Interview in *Time*
magazine, March 15, 2004.

The publishers would like to thank Rosie
Nixon, Charly Rimsa, Sarah Williams, Marie
Lorimer, and Nicola Hodgson for their
assistance in the preparation of this book.

Disclaimer: This book is not authorized or
approved by Johnny Depp.

All the Internet addresses (URLs) given in this
book were valid at the time of going to press.
However, due to the dynamic nature of the
Internet, some addresses may have changed, or
sites may have ceased to exist since
publication. While the author and publishers
regret any inconvenience this may cause
readers, no responsibility for any such changes
can be accepted by either the author or the
publishers.

Contents

Any words appearing in the text in bold, **like this**, are explained in the glossary. You can also look out for them in the Star words box at the bottom of each page.

Who Is the Real Johnny Depp?

ALL ABOUT JOHNNY

Full name: John Christopher Depp II
Born: June 9, 1963
Place of birth: Owensboro, Kentucky
Family: Father: John; mother: Betty Sue; brother: Dan; half-sisters: Debbie and Christie
Height: 5 feet, 10 inches (1.77 meters)
Relationships: Married Lori Allison (1983–85). Lived with Sherilyn Fenn, Jennifer Grey, Winona Ryder, and Kate Moss. Now lives with Vanessa Paradis (1998–).
Children: Lily-Rose Melody (born 1999); John Christopher Depp III, known as Jack (born 2002)
Big break: Appearing as a detective, Tommy Hanson, in the television series *21 Jump Street* (1987)
Interests: Playing guitar, collecting things, hanging out with his family

Johnny Depp has played many roles. He has been a pirate, a detective, and a writer—to name just a few of his many screen characters. So, what is the real Johnny like?

> " I do what I want. I won't be a slave to success. "

Johnny likes to play unusual roles such as Edward Scissorhands.

Star words   director person in charge of making a movie

Johnny is photographed wherever he goes.

Johnny the rebel

Johnny is not the usual kind of screen star. Despite his good looks, he hardly ever chooses glamorous roles. Instead, he often plays **oddball** characters. Johnny says he likes playing outsiders. He thinks that they are more like him.

Not just an actor

Acting is not Johnny's only interest. His first love is music. He says he wants his life to be filled with different experiences.

Find out later

In which movie does Johnny meet a headless horseman?

Which comedian is Johnny a fan of?

Which **director** has Johnny worked with four times?

Young Johnny

Family tattoos

Johnny has a Betty Sue tattoo on his left arm. It shows his mom's name inside a red heart. On his right arm is the name of his son, Jack. Over his heart is his daughter's name, Lily-Rose.

Johnny spent his early years in Kentucky. His father was a city engineer in the town of Owensboro. His mother, Betty Sue, worked as a waitress in a local coffee shop.

The Depp family did not have a lot of money to spare. They lived in an ordinary house in an ordinary town, just like many other families across the country.

A close family

When he was growing up, Johnny was very close to his mother. He also spent as much time as he could with his grandfather. Johnny's special name for his grandfather was Pawpaw.

Young Johnny followed Pawpaw everywhere. He even worked beside him, picking crops in the fields. Johnny was only seven years old when Pawpaw died. He missed his grandfather very badly.

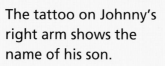

The tattoo on Johnny's right arm shows the name of his son.

Star fact

Johnny believes in ghosts. Sometimes he feels his grandfather's ghost watching over him.

Star words

Cherokee member of a Native American people that used to live in most of the southern United States

Youngest in the family

Johnny was the youngest in his family. He has two half-sisters—Debbie and Christie—and a brother named Dan. Now, Christie and Dan both work with Johnny. Christie is Johnny's manager and adviser. Dan is Johnny's partner in a **movie production company**.

Johnny used to help his grandfather pick crops in Kentucky.

Cherokee ancestors

Johnny's grandfather came from a Native American family. Pawpaw's ancestors belonged to the **Cherokee** tribe. Johnny's dark coloring and high cheekbones show that that he has Cherokee blood.

Johnny is still close to his mother.

movie production company business that makes movies to earn money

Daredevil hero

When Johnny was growing up, one of his heroes was Evel Knievel (below). Evel Knievel was a daring stuntman who performed amazing motorcycle jumps. Once, he jumped over a row of thirteen double-decker buses. Evel Knievel often crash-landed and broke many bones.

Moving to Florida

When Johnny was eight years old, his family moved to Florida. His father, John, worked in Miramar, a small town north of Miami. The family did not like living in Miramar, but had to stay there because of John's job.

Johnny and his family never really settled in Miramar. They kept on moving from place to place. Most of the time, they lived in **motel** rooms.

All the Depp children were unhappy in Florida. Each time they moved, they had to get to know a new group of friends. In the end, Johnny stopped trying to make new friends.

Odd one out

Johnny did not do well in school. He did not try in his classes and was a **rebel** and a daredevil. He was different from the other children.

❝ I was not the most popular kid at school. I always felt like a total freak. ❞

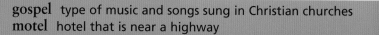

Star words

gospel type of music and songs sung in Christian churches
motel hotel that is near a highway

He hated most of the popular television shows. Instead, he watched old movies about World War II. He also spent a lot of time on his own, digging tunnels and thinking up "great escapes."

Learning from the preacher

On Sundays Johnny's family went to hear his uncle preach at a nearby church. Johnny's uncle ran a popular **gospel** group. Johnny loved to watch his uncle stand up on the stage and perform. He decided that he would be a performer when he grew up.

This is a self-portrait of Van Gogh.

Johnny took ideas from movies such as *The Great Escape*.

Wild artist

While Johnny was living in Florida, he became interested in Vincent van Gogh. Van Gogh was a 19th-century painter who created an emotional style of his own. Johnny admired Van Gogh for being a great artist as well as a rebel and a loner.

rebel someone who questions the rules and does not follow everyone else

Getting into music

By the time he was twelve years old, Johnny felt his life was not going well. Then, his mom bought him a special present. She spent $25 on an electric guitar. From then on, Johnny spent hours locked in his bedroom. He was determined to learn to play the guitar.

Johnny taught himself to play by listening to records and repeating what he heard. His two favorite bands were the Sex Pistols and U2. The Sex Pistols were a leading punk rock group. U2 made a different type of music called New Wave. Johnny's aim was to create a sound that was a blend of the two different styles.

> " All I wanted since I was twelve years old was to join a band and go on the road. "

Punk rock

Punk rock started in the late 1970s. It was meant to shock and even frighten people. Punk bands made loud, raw, angry music. Most of their songs were violent attacks on modern **society**.

The Sex Pistols were a famous punk band.

Star words   society all the different groups of people in a country

The Irish band U2 made songs with a powerful message.

Flame

Soon, Johnny was ready to form his own band. The band was called Flame, and it wrote its own music. Most of the time the band members just practiced in a garage, but sometimes they played local shows. Later, the band changed its name to The Kids.

Johnny designed the costumes for Flame. At first, the band wore simple T-shirts that said "Flame." Then, they wore plain shirts. Then, they started to wear more exciting costumes, such as crushed velvet shirts and bell-bottom pants. Johnny found most of these clothes in his mother's closet.

New Wave

New Wave music began at the same time as punk rock. It had a different sound from punk, but it still had a powerful message. Elvis Costello, Blondie, and Talking Heads were all part of the New Wave movement.

Iggy Pop

Iggy Pop is sometimes called the grandfather of punk rock. He began performing in the 1960s with his band The Stooges. He has also appeared in over fifteen movies. Iggy had a small part in *Cry Baby*, one of Johnny's first movies.

Johnny and Iggy Pop together at the Cannes Film Festival.

Tough times

When Johnny was fifteen, his parents divorced and the family split up. His father and sister Debbie moved to a different town. The rest of the family stayed with Betty Sue.

It was a very hard time for Johnny. He hated school. He also worried about his mom, who was very upset about the divorce. The one good thing in his life was his music. The Kids were starting to be a success. They had begun to play in local clubs.

 **Star fact**

When he played for The Kids, Johnny usually earned about $25 a day. Now, he can earn a thousand times that much.

Star words   opening band   band that performs at the beginning of a show, usually before a more famous band comes on stage

Johnny still plays in a band today.

The Kids take off

At the age of sixteen, Johnny dropped out of school. He concentrated on writing songs and playing with The Kids. The band began to play in clubs all over Florida. Sometimes The Kids worked as the **opening band** for famous music acts. The band played on the same stage as the B52s, Talking Heads, and Iggy Pop.

Early marriage

Around this time Johnny met Lori Allison. She was a makeup artist and a great fan of The Kids. Johnny and Lori fell in love. They got married when he was 20 and she was 25. Lori believed that The Kids had a great future. She worked very hard to try to help make the band a success.

Too young?

Looking back, Johnny thinks he got married too young. "I had the right intentions," he says, "but the wrong timing."

Starting Out

City of Angels

Los Angeles is not just famous for Hollywood. It is also a major music center. Every year, hundreds of young bands arrive in LA. They all hope to get noticed by the city's record companies and **music producers**. Only a handful ever succeed.

In 1984 The Kids moved to Los Angeles. The band members hoped that this was their chance to make it really big. Life was hard in LA, though. There were just too many bands trying to succeed.

Trying to survive

The band was not a big success, and there was not enough money to pay the bills. All the members of The Kids were forced to get other jobs. Johnny worked at lots of low-paying jobs.

It was also a hard time for Johnny and Lori. They both realized they were drifting apart. In the end, they agreed that it would be best to split up. The couple got divorced when Johnny was 22.

The Kids moved to Los Angeles to try to make it big!

Star words

agent someone who works for actors or other performers and tries to find them jobs

A lucky break

Just before Johnny and Lori split up, they went to meet an old friend of Lori's. This friend was the actor Nicolas Cage. By that time, Nicolas had already been in lots of movies.

Nicolas liked Johnny's spiky-haired, punk-rock image. He thought that Johnny would look good on screen. He suggested that Johnny should meet his **agent**. It was Johnny's first move into the world of acting.

Nicolas Cage

Nicolas Cage is one of Hollywood's leading actors. He has acted in comedies, thrillers, and action movies. In 2002 he starred in *Adaptation* (below), where he played two parts: a **screenwriter** and his imaginary brother.

music producer someone who decides how a piece of music or a song will sound when it is being recorded

A Nightmare on Elm Street

Thanks to Nicolas Cage, Johnny went to meet the movie **director** Wes Craven. He was making a horror movie called *A Nightmare on Elm Street*. Craven was looking for someone to play the part of Glen Lantz. As soon as he saw Johnny, Craven knew he had found the right man. He could see that Johnny had star quality.

The next step

After *Nightmare*, Johnny had a couple of parts in television movies. He also starred in a teen comedy called *Private Resort*. Johnny hated the movie—and so did the **critics**. Around this time, Johnny decided he needed some acting training, so he enrolled at the Loft Studio. This was a drama school where actors learned techniques such as **voice control**. After his studies at the Loft, Johnny was a much better actor, but he still did not have many jobs.

Soldier boy

Then, one day, Johnny got a call from director Oliver Stone. Stone was planning a movie about the Vietnam War called *Platoon*. He thought that Johnny could play the young soldier Private Lerner.

Oliver Stone is a very famous director. He has made many successful movies.

⭐ Star fact

In *Platoon* Johnny wears a helmet with "Sherilyn" painted on it. At that time, he was dating the actress Sherilyn Fenn.

Star words

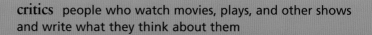

critics people who watch movies, plays, and other shows and write what they think about them

> *Platoon* was praised for showing the Vietnam War in a very realistic way.

Platoon is based on Stone's own experiences in Vietnam. It stars Charlie Sheen, Tom Berenger, and Willem Dafoe. Critics loved the movie and praised Johnny's performance.

> *Platoon* was shot in the thick jungle of the Philippines.

Jungle training

Oliver Stone is a brilliant but tough director. He made all the actors in *Platoon* train in the jungle for two weeks. The training included a 60-mile (97-kilometer) march. Many of the actors suffered from insect bites and fever.

voice control ways of making actors' voices stronger and clearer

Cops in schools

21 Jump Street was based on a real police experiment. In 1974 a group of officers pretended to be students in Los Angeles schools. They arrested several young drug dealers. Many people objected to the experiment, however, and it was dropped.

Officer Tom

Soon after he had finished filming *Platoon*, Johnny was offered a part in a television series. The series was *21 Jump Street*. It followed the adventures of a group of undercover detectives who worked in a high school. The **director** wanted Johnny to play the part of Officer Tom Hanson, one of the leading young detectives.

Right from the start, Johnny was not eager to play Officer Tom. He hated the idea of detectives in schools. Johnny turned down the role twice, but the director kept asking him. In the end, Johnny decided he needed the work. He signed up for thirteen episodes.

Teen idol

21 Jump Street was a huge success, and Johnny became a teenage **idol**. Girls all across the United States fell in love with his character, Officer Tom. Every month Johnny's face appeared on the covers of teen magazines.

Johnny in character as Officer Tom.

Star words   idol someone who is looked up to or admired by lots of people

He also got bag-loads of fan mail. None of this made Johnny happy, though. He hated being **idolized** for his looks.

Long-running show

Johnny stayed with *21 Jump Street* for three years. He even moved to Vancouver in Canada, where the series was being filmed. By the end of his three years, Johnny was very restless. He was desperate to try a more challenging role.

> ❝ I was this product. Teen Boy. Poster Boy. All that stuff that I wasn't. ❞

Fishy friend

When Johnny was filming *21 Jump Street*, he was visited by Sal Jenco, one of his few high-school friends. Sal did his usual trick of puffing out his cheeks like a blowfish. Sal was asked to join the show—and play a character named Blowfish.

21 Jump Street made Johnny a "pin-up."

idolized worshipped or loved

Sherilyn and Jennifer

While he was working on *21 Jump Street*, Johnny got engaged twice. The first time was to actress Sherilyn Fenn. Sherilyn later starred in the television series *Twin Peaks*.

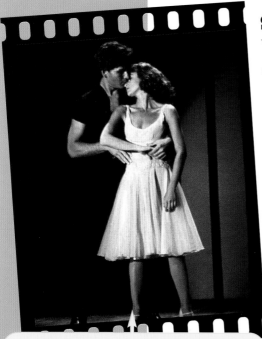

Jennifer costarred with Patrick Swayze in the hit movie *Dirty Dancing*.

Johnny's second engagement was to Jennifer Grey. Jennifer played the lead in *Dirty Dancing*. The movie was a great success and made Jennifer a star.

Neither of Johnny's engagements lasted very long. Johnny had to spend long periods of time in Canada filming *21 Jump Street*. This made it hard to hold a relationship together. Johnny was searching for the right woman, but he had not found her yet.

John Waters

Johnny is a great fan of director John Waters. Waters makes "bad taste" movies that deal with "tacky" parts of **society**. His movie *Hairspray* tells the story of a group of teenage **celebrities** and their mothers. It was also made into a hit musical.

Return to the big screen

In 1989 **director** John Waters offered Johnny a great movie role. He wanted Johnny to play the hero in his movie *Cry Baby*. The film is set in the 1950s. It tells the story of Cry Baby Walker, a teenage heartthrob who hangs around with a very bad crowd. Cry Baby only has to shed one tear to make all the girls fall in love with him. Johnny loved playing Cry Baby. It gave him the chance to get back into movies. It also made fun of his real-life role as a teenage heartthrob.

Star words   celebrity famous person

James Dean lookalike

In his role as Cry Baby, Johnny reminded many people of another young star. James Dean (above) was a teenage **idol** in the 1950s. Just like Johnny, James Dean was famous for combining stunning good looks with great acting talent.

Johnny's looks made him perfect for the role of Cry Baby Walker.

Highs and Lows

Tim Burton

Tim Burton began his career by directing horror movies. His first big break came when he directed the **black comedy** *Beetlejuice*. Many of Burton's movies mix fantasy and comedy. *Batman* is one of his most famous movies.

★ ★ ★ ★

In 1990 the **director** Tim Burton offered Johnny an exciting role. He asked Johnny to star in his movie *Edward Scissorhands*. Burton had already made his name with the **blockbuster** *Batman*. This meant he had plenty of money to spend on his next project. He wanted to make a great movie, and he wanted Johnny to be its star.

Strange story

Tim Burton had the idea for *Edward Scissorhands* when he was very young. He imagined the story of a strange inventor who created a boy with hedge-clipper hands. *Edward Scissorhands* is a brilliant mixture of dark fantasy and comedy. Some **critics** called it a modern fairy tale.

Movies

Johnny has been in four Tim Burton movies:

Edward Scissorhands (1988)

Ed Wood (1994)

Sleepy Hollow (1999)

Charlie and the Chocolate Factory (2005)

Johnny and Tim Burton enjoy working together.

Star words   black comedy mixture of comedy with a serious, sometimes horrible, story

Great actors

Johnny was not the only star in *Edward Scissorhands*. The movie also featured Vincent Price and Winona Ryder. Vincent, a famous horror actor, played Edward's weird inventor. Winona took the part of Kim, the girl who falls in love with Edward. At the time that they were filming *Edward Scissorhands*, Johnny and Winona were dating. This could have been awkward, but Tim Burton says it was never a problem. "They were very **professional**," he says. "They didn't bring any weird stuff to the set."

Sad hero

Johnny loved playing Edward Scissorhands. He was **fascinated** by the idea of a character who "wants to touch but can't."

Boris Karloff played Frankenstein's monster in a famous old movie of the story.

Monsters?

Edward Scissorhands has a connection with the tale of Frankenstein. In both stories, a weird inventor gives life to a strange creature. Frankenstein's creation is always seen as a monster. Edward is kind-hearted, but his strange appearance means that people are afraid of him.

fascinated very interested
professional focused on work

Winona Ryder

Winona Ryder made her name as an actress in the **black comedy** *Beetlejuice*. She likes to take challenging roles and has starred in such varied movies as *Little Women* and *Girl, Interrupted*.

Johnny and Winona

Johnny and Winona first met in 1989. Winona was only seventeen years old, but she had already been in several movies. Johnny was 26. They were both talented and good-looking, and they clicked immediately.

After they had been dating for five months, Johnny gave Winona an engagement ring. A month later, they were living together. They tried to spend as much time together as they could, but they did not plan to marry right away.

⭐ Star fact

Johnny once sent Winona 200 helium balloons. They filled a whole room!

Most of the time, Johnny and Winona were very happy, but sometimes things got difficult. They both worked very long hours, and everywhere they went they were followed by the press.

In the end, the pressure got to be too much. They also began to realize that they were drifting apart. By 1993 Johnny's relationship with Winona was over.

Johnny and Winona were photographed everywhere they went.

Star words

eccentric someone with unusual interests who does not fit in easily with other people

New directions

Around the time that Johnny and Winona were splitting up, Johnny accepted another unusual movie role. He was ready for a new challenge in his acting career.

Benny and Joon

In the movie *Benny and Joon*, Johnny plays Sam, a strange, clown-like character. Sam is an **eccentric** who cannot read. He expresses himself by performing silent comedy acts.

Sam's acts are based on the silent movies of Buster Keaton. Johnny studied these movies for hours on end. He tried out all Keaton's tricks and falls—and ended up with lots of bruises!

Silent star

Buster Keaton (above) was one of the greatest stars of silent movies. Like Charlie Chaplin, he made comedies in which he got into endless scrapes. Buster had trained as an acrobat and did all his own stunts.

The character of Sam gets into some scrapes performing his comedy acts!

Small-town life

The town of Endora in *Gilbert Grape* does not really exist, but it is typical of thousands of small towns across the country. Johnny knows this kind of town very well. He has compared Endora to the town of Miramar, Florida, where he grew up.

Gilbert Grape

After *Benny and Joon*, Johnny's next major movie was *What's Eating Gilbert Grape?* In this movie, Johnny plays the part of Gilbert, a young man stuck in a small town.

Gilbert has a dead-end job and a problem family to support. His mother is extremely overweight and never leaves the house. His father is dead, and his brother, Arnie, has serious problems that affect his behavior.

Into this unhappy life comes young Becky. She offers Gilbert the chance to escape. In the end, he has to choose between his family and his freedom.

Gilbert tries to take care of his brother, Arnie, played by Leonardo DiCaprio.

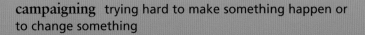

Star words

campaigning trying hard to make something happen or to change something

Playing himself?

Some people say that Johnny played himself when he played Gilbert. Johnny does not agree, but he does admit that there are **"parallels"** between his life and Gilbert's. After his parents split up, Johnny had to take care of his mother. They had very little money and he felt trapped in a boring town. "Sometimes you play roles that you are close to," says Johnny. "You **identify** with the guy."

Young Leo

Leonardo DiCaprio played the part of Gilbert's brother. Leo was nineteen years old when he played Arnie. He had been appearing in movies since he was fourteen.

During filming, Leo and Johnny spent a lot of time together. Later, Leo said it was just like being brothers.

> Johnny's hard to figure out. But that makes him interesting. (Leonardo DiCaprio)

Leonardo DiCaprio

After he appeared in *Gilbert Grape*, Leonardo DiCaprio's movie career took off. In two years he was playing the lead in *Romeo and Juliet*. Now, Leo (below) has made many successful movies. He also spends time **campaigning** to save the environment.

identify recognize or relate to
parallels things that are similar or the same

Johnny and Kate

A few months after Johnny and Winona split up, Johnny met English supermodel Kate Moss in a New York cafe. They started to go out almost immediately. Even though Johnny was eleven years older than Kate, they got along really well. Johnny liked Kate's English sense of humor, and they had a lot of fun together.

At that time, photos of Kate were everywhere. This did not mean that Kate was big-headed, though. Johnny loved the fact that she was down-to-earth.

Kate Moss

Kate Moss is one of the world's best-known fashion models. She is famous for her slender frame and striking, **waiflike** looks. Kate has worked for all the big designers, including Calvin Klein and Yves Saint Laurent.

Kate and Johnny made a stunning couple.

Star words   waiflike very fragile in appearance

Stormy scenes

Kate and Johnny had a stormy relationship. Sometimes they had big arguments and separated for a while. Then, they would get back together again and everything was fine. One major problem for Johnny and Kate was the press. Photographers loved to spot the glamorous couple. Several times, Johnny lost his temper with them.

One night, Johnny had a disagreement with a security guard at the hotel where he was staying. Johnny got so worked up that he trashed a hotel room. He was arrested and held in a cell for 48 hours. This was a low point in his life. Later, he tried to explain, "I'm human and I get angry like everybody else."

Weird roles?

Over the next few years, Johnny kept on working hard. Most of the parts he played were **oddball** characters. Usually the **critics** loved his movies, but not everyone was impressed. Some people thought he should stop picking such weird roles.

" I just do the roles I like. I hate the obvious stuff. I don't respond to it. "

Fairy-tale house

While he was going out with Kate, Johnny found an amazing house (below). It looked like a fairy-tale castle. Johnny knew right away that he had to buy it. Now, it is his home whenever he works in Hollywood.

29

Johnny the Star

In the late 1990s, Johnny played some very popular roles. He continued playing unusual characters, but some of his movies appealed to more people than before.

Sleepy Hollow

One of the big movie successes of 1999 was *Sleepy Hollow*. The movie is based on a famous story by Washington Irving. Tim Burton **directed** the film. It was Johnny's third movie with him.

In *Sleepy Hollow*, Johnny plays Constable Ichabod Crane. He is sent to investigate a murder committed by a headless horseman. For most of the movie, Crane is scared out of his mind. It is the kind of role that Johnny really enjoys. He gave a very exciting performance.

★ ★ ★ ★ ★ ★ ★ ★ ★ ★ ★

Washington Irving

The author Washington Irving (above) lived from 1783 to 1859. In addition to writing *The Legend of Sleepy Hollow*, he also wrote the tale of Rip Van Winkle, a man who slept for twenty years.

★ ★ ★ ★ ★ ★ ★ ★ ★ ★ ★

Constable Crane is a bit of an **oddball**!

★ **Star words**   soundtrack music for a movie

French actress Juliette Binoche played opposite Johnny in *Chocolat*.

Chocolat

The year after *Sleepy Hollow* appeared, Johnny took a minor role in *Chocolat*. In this lighthearted movie, he plays a traveling guitar player. Johnny only appears on screen for seventeen minutes, but some people nonetheless think he was the star.

Some of Johnny's fans were surprised that he chose such a romantic part, but the character obviously appealed to him. It also gave him the chance to play his guitar on screen.

★ Star fact

Johnny plays the first and last songs on the **soundtrack** for *Chocolat*.

Chocolate roles

Chocolat is not Johnny's only movie featuring chocolate. He also plays Willy Wonka, the owner of the factory in *Charlie and the Chocolate Factory*. Luckily, Johnny loves chocolate. He especially likes milk chocolate footballs.

31

Pirates of the Caribbean

So far, Johnny's most **high-profile** role is Captain Jack Sparrow from *Pirates of the Caribbean*. The movie is based on a Disneyland ride and is aimed at all ages. One of the reasons Johnny chose to star in *Pirates* was because his children could enjoy watching the movie.

Keith Richards

Keith Richards (above) is a good friend of Johnny's. He has been in the Rolling Stones since 1962. Now, Johnny has persuaded Keith to try acting as well. Keith will play Captain Jack's father in the sequel to *Pirates*.

Johnny's performance as Captain Jack was very unusual—but it worked!

Johnny's daughter, Lily-Rose, was four years old when he made *Pirates*. Johnny took her to watch him filming some of the scenes. Johnny says that Lily-Rose loved his costume. "She really liked the teeth and all the stuff dangling in my hair," he says. "She thinks her daddy is a real pirate."

Star words   high-profile getting lots of attention

Captain Jack

Pirates of the Caribbean is a classic storybook adventure, but Captain Jack is not the usual storybook pirate. Johnny based the character of Captain Jack on Keith Richards, of the rock group the Rolling Stones.

Finding Neverland

Pirates of the Caribbean is not Johnny's only movie featuring pirates. In *Finding Neverland*, Johnny plays James Barrie, the author of *Peter Pan*. The movie shows how Barrie got his ideas for the story of Peter and the scary pirate Captain Hook.

★ Star fact

Johnny was **nominated** for an Oscar for his roles as Captain Jack Sparrow and James Barrie.

Rejected roles

Johnny always insists that he is not "blockbuster boy." Here are a few of the big roles that he has turned down:

Robin Hood in Robin Hood Prince of Thieves (taken by Kevin Costner)

Lestat in Interview with a Vampire (taken by Tom Cruise)

Dracula in Bram Stoker's Dracula (taken by Gary Oldman)

Officer Jack Traven in Speed (taken by Keanu Reeves)

Johnny playing James Barrie, who is acting like a pirate in this scene from *Finding Neverland*.

Family Life

Vanessa the musician

Vanessa Paradis was born in Paris, France, and first shot to fame when she was only fourteen years old. In 1986 her song *"Joe le Taxi"* became an international hit. Over the next six years, she made three albums. In 2000 Vanessa released a new album called *Bliss*.

Johnny is now in a happy, long-term relationship with Vanessa Paradis. The couple first met in 1998 while Johnny was filming in Paris. Johnny spotted Vanessa in a hotel. He asked her to join him at his table. A few months later, they were sharing an apartment in Paris.

Johnny was 35 and had reached a stage in his life when he wanted to settle down. He dreamed of having children of his own. When he met Vanessa, Johnny soon discovered that she shared his dream.

Vanessa Paradis

Vanessa is a singer, actress, and model. She released her first hit song when she was just fourteen. At the age of seventeen, she made her first movie. Over the next ten years she appeared in four more movies. By the time Vanessa met Johnny, she had also made her mark in the fashion world. In 1991 she became the new face in ads for a famous perfume.

Lily-Rose and Jack

In May 1999 Johnny and Vanessa had their first child. They named her Lily-Rose Melody. Their son, Jack, was born three years later. Johnny says that having children is the best thing that ever happened to him.

> They say life begins at 40, but for me it began at 35. That was the year I started my family.

John Christopher Depp III

Johnny's son is named John Christopher Depp III, after his father and grandfather. Nobody ever calls him John, though. He is always known as Jack.

Vanessa and Johnny keep their children away from the press, but the couple is often seen out together.

Family first

Johnny tries to spend as much time as he can with Vanessa and his children. Most of all, he likes to stay at home, having fun with Lily-Rose and Jack.

Johnny and Vanessa have three homes: an apartment in Paris, a house in Hollywood, and a house in the south of France. Usually they live in France. The Depp family home is a large villa in the French countryside, close to St. Tropez.

Harry Houdini

The great magician Harry Houdini (above) lived from 1874 to 1926. Houdini was famous for his daring escape acts. He could even escape from a locked trunk placed under water. Johnny has always been **fascinated** by Houdini.

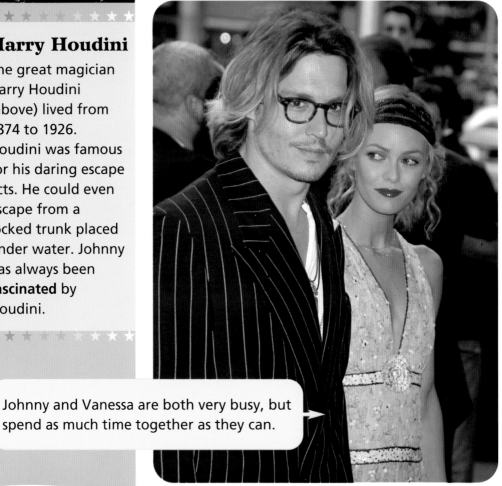

Johnny and Vanessa are both very busy, but spend as much time together as they can.

People from the local village often see Johnny shopping in the market. Johnny sometimes stops to talk—his French is now quite good. Sometimes Johnny joins the old men of the village for a friendly game of *boules*, a game in which you roll balls at a target on the ground.

> **These days, I just play Barbies and hang out with the kiddies.**

Staying private

Johnny is determined to keep his family life out of the public eye. He wants his children to have a happy childhood—without the attention of the press.

Johnny the collector

Johnny loves collecting things. In the past, he used to collect lizards and snakes. Nowadays, he mainly collects paintings and old books. Johnny also has a collection of old locks. He started collecting locks after he became interested in the magician Harry Houdini.

Some of the things that Johnny collects are a little odd. He used to have a model of a life-sized yellow gorilla.

Likes/dislikes

Johnny likes:
Bugs
Snakes
Lizards
Funny hats

Johnny dislikes:
Spiders
Clowns

Other Interests

Johnny's first love has always been music. Ever since he was twelve years old, he has played the guitar. Johnny formed his first band when he was thirteen, and he still plays in a band today.

Johnny has many friends in the music business. One of his friends is Noel Gallagher, from the band Oasis. Johnny also loves to play his guitar with Keith Richards of the Rolling Stones.

> I never really wanted to be an actor . . . I was a musician and still am.

Playing for Oasis

In 1997 Johnny played a **slide guitar** solo on the song "Fade In-Out" on the Oasis album *Be Here Now.* Noel Gallagher asked Johnny to play it for him because it was too hard for Noel to play himself.

Johnny got to play the guitar in the movie *Chocolat*.

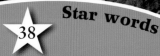

A band called P

In 1993 Johnny and some friends formed a band called P. Other famous members include Flea from the Red Hot Chilli Peppers and Johnny's old friend Sal Jenco. The band still plays together whenever it can. In 1995 P released its first album.

Johnny gave his friend Noel Gallagher a white guitar with the letter "P" on it. Noel often uses this guitar at Oasis shows.

Noel Gallagher of Oasis asked Johnny to play on Oasis's album.

More music

Johnny has appeared in lots of music videos. He played alongside Iggy Pop in one of his recent shows. He has also **directed** several music videos for Vanessa Paradis.

On Vanessa's album *Bliss*, Johnny plays lead guitar on two of the songs. He also wrote the album's title song with Vanessa.

Soundtracks

In 2003 Johnny wrote part of the music **soundtrack** for *Once upon a Time in Mexico* (below). In this movie, Johnny plays the part of a **corrupt** CIA agent. Johnny wrote the theme tune for his character.

Fast laughs

Some of Johnny's best roles have been comic creations. He loves **quirky**, "off-the-wall" comedy. His all-time favorite television show is the British comedy *The Fast Show*. *The Fast Show* only lasted for three seasons, but millions of people loved its crazy characters.

The last laugh

Johnny used to take tapes of *The Fast Show* with him when he was filming. He has become good friends with Paul Whitehouse, one of the show's creators and stars. Johnny appeared on the last ever sketch of *The Fast Show*. He played himself in a comic sketch called "Suits you." Paul Whitehouse appeared with Johnny again—this time on the big screen. He has a small part in the movie *Finding Neverland*.

Island home

Johnny made one of his childhood dreams come true when he bought his own island! The 35-acre island in the Bahamas cost about three million dollars. It has six beaches, its own harbor, lots of palm trees, and a lagoon.

Johnny is a big fan of comedian Paul Whitehouse.

Star words

jet set people who have a lot of money and who often fly from one country to another

Star fact

Johnny loves Dr. Seuss's *Cat in the Hat*. He says the Cat gave him the idea to start wearing funny hats.

Mister Stench

Johnny has always had an **offbeat** sense of humor. When he was eight years old, he chose the nickname "Mister Stench" for himself.

A modest star

Johnny is asked to appear on talk shows all the time, but he almost always says no. He only takes part in things that he really believes in.

A restaurant in Paris

Today, Johnny is branching out in other directions. With his actor friends Sean Penn and John Malkovich, he has bought a restaurant in Paris. The restaurant is called the Man Ray after a famous photographer, painter, and sculptor. It has become a favorite with the Paris **jet set**.

Like his choice of roles, Johnny's sense of style is pretty unusual.

offbeat   unusual, not what people expect
quirky   strange or funny

New Directions

Johnny the director

In 1996 Johnny directed *The Brave*, a story of a Native American. He also wrote the script with his brother, Dan. *The Brave* was not a success, but some **critics** said that Johnny should try directing again.

What does the future hold for Johnny? He wants to widen his range of roles. He has tried movie **directing** once, and he will probably try it again. He will certainly stay involved in the world of music. Only one thing is certain: he will keep surprising everyone.

Different roles

Johnny plans to make more movies that his children can enjoy. He plays the crazy inventor Willy Wonka in *Charlie and the Chocolate Factory*. He will also return as Captain Jack Sparrow in *Pirates of the Caribbean 2: Dead Man's Chest*.

> I miss Captain Jack. I'm looking forward to meeting him again.

Charlie and the Chocolate Factory is a movie that Johnny's children can watch and enjoy.

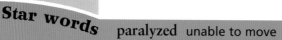

Star words   paralyzed unable to move

Johnny's voice will soon be heard in an animated movie called *The Corpse Bride*. Meanwhile, he has taken on a challenging role in *The Diving Bell and the Butterfly*. In this unusual movie, Johnny will play a totally **paralyzed** patient who visits imaginary places in his mind.

Future awards?

During his career, Johnny has been **nominated** for four Golden Globe awards. He has also been nominated for two Oscars—one for his role in *Pirates of the Caribbean* and the other for *Finding Neverland*. So far, though, Johnny has not won any of these big awards.

Surely this will change in the future. Sooner or later, Hollywood must recognize the **unique** talents of Johnny Depp.

Johnny has already been honored with a star on the Walk of Fame in Hollywood.

unique only one

43

Find Out More

Books to read

Goodall, Nigel. *Johnny Depp: The Biography*. London: Blake, 1999.

Goodall, Nigel. *What's Eating Johnny Depp? An Intimate Biography*. North Pomfret, Vt.: Trafalgar Square, 2004.

Heard, Christopher. *Depp*. Toronto, Can.: ECW, 2001.

Higgins, Kara. *Johnny Depp: People in the News*. San Diego, Calif.: Lucent Books, 2004.

Hunter, Jack. *Johnny Depp: Movie Top Ten*. London: Creation, 2000.

Robb, Brian J. *Johnny Depp: A Modern Rebel*. London: Plexus, 2004.

Filmography

Charlie and the Chocolate Factory (2005)
Secret Window (2004)
The Libertine (2004)
Finding Neverland (2004)
Once Upon a Time in Mexico (2003)
Pirates of the Caribbean: The Curse of the Black Pearl (2003)
Lost in LaMancha (2002)
From Hell (2001)
Blow (2001)
Chocolat (2000)
Before Night Falls (2000)
The Man Who Cried (2000)
Sleepy Hollow (1999)
The Ninth Gate (1999)
The Astronaut's Wife (1999)
Fear and Loathing in Las Vegas (1998)
LA Without a Map (1998)
Cannes Man (1996)
The Brave (1996)
Donnie Brasco (1996)
Nick of Time (1995)
Dead Man (1995)
Don Juan DeMarco (1995)
Ed Wood (1994)

Benny and Joon (1993)
What's Eating Gilbert Grape? (1993)
Arizona Dream (1991)
Freddy's Dead: The Final Nightmare (1991)
Cry Baby (1990)
Edward Scissorhands (1990)
21 Jump Street (television series, 1987–90)
Platoon (1986)
Private Resort (1985)
Nightmare on Elm Street (1984)

Music videos and albums

Que fait la vie? by Vanessa Paradis (director) (2001)
Pourtant by Vanessa Paradis (director) (2001)
"Fade In-Out" track on *Be Here Now* album by
  Oasis (1997)
"That Woman's Got Me Drinking" by Shane McGowan
  and the Pogues (guest appearance and director) (1994)
"Stuff" by John Frusciante (director) (1993)
"It's a Shame about Ray" by Lemonheads
  (guest appearance) (1991)
"Into the Great Wide Open" by Tom Petty
  (guest appearance) (1991)
"Joey" by Concrete Blond (guest appearance) (1990)

Websites

Explore the Internet to find out more about Johnny
Depp.

There are billions of pages on the Internet, so it can be
difficult to find exactly what you are looking for. A
search engine looks through the entire web and lists all
the sites that match the words in the search box. It can
give thousands of links, but the best matches are at the
top of the list, on the first page. Try google.com.

Glossary

agent someone who works for actors or other performers and tries to find them jobs

black comedy mixture of comedy with a serious, sometimes horrible, story

blockbuster movie that does really well and earns lots of money

campaigning trying hard to make something happen or to change something

celebrity famous person

Cherokee member of a Native American people that used to live in most of the southern United States

corrupt dishonest

critics people who watch movies, plays, and other shows and write what they think about them

director person in charge of making a movie

eccentric someone with unusual interests who does not fit in easily with other people

fascinated very interested

gospel type of music and songs sung in Christian churches

high-profile getting lots of attention

identify recognize or relate to

idol someone who is looked up to or admired by lots of people

idolized worshipped or loved

jet set people who have a lot of money and who often fly from one country to another

motel hotel that is near a highway

movie production company business that makes movies to earn money

music producer someone who decides how a piece of music or a song will sound when it is being recorded

nominated chosen as one of the people who might win an award

oddball unusual

offbeat unusual, not what people expect

opening band band that performs at the beginning of a show, usually before a more famous band comes on stage

parallels things that are similar or the same

paralyzed unable to move

professional focused on work

quirky strange or funny

rebel someone who questions the rules and does not follow everyone else

screenwriter someone who writes the stories, or scripts, for movies and television shows

slide guitar style of guitar playing. The guitarist wears a piece of metal (called a bottleneck) on his or her finger and slides this over the strings to make a new sound.

society all the different groups of people in a country

soundtrack music for a movie

unique only one

voice control ways of making actors' voices stronger and clearer

waiflike very fragile in appearance

Index